# All About Mopeds

# All About Mopeds

BY MAX ALTH
illustrated by Michael Horen

A Concise Guide

FRANKLIN WATTS | NEW YORK | LONDON | 1978

Photos courtesy of Vespa: pp. x and 11;
Motobecane America, Ltd.: pp. 3 and 19.

Library of Congress Cataloging in Publication Data

Alth, Max, 1917–
    All about mopeds.

    (A Concise guide)
    Includes index.
    SUMMARY: A comprehensive guide to the pur-
chase, operation, and maintenance of a moped, a
light-weight motorized bicycle.
    1. Mopeds—Juvenile literature.    [1. Mopeds]
I. Horen, Michael.    II. Title.
TL443.A47              629.22′72              78–2348
ISBN 0–531–01496–7

# Contents

Dedicated to

Char
Syme
Misch
Michael
Arabella
Mendel

and everyone else
who is at least
young at heart.

# All About Mopeds

# 1

## Why Moped?

For the fun of it.

If you can imagine yourself whizzing down a country road, through woods, or going to school on a bicycle you don't have to pedal except when going up very steep hills; if you can picture a vehicle that can travel 75 to 200 and more miles (120 to 322 km) on a single gallon of gasoline, then you have a fair picture of the fun you can have and the foot slogging you can save with a moped.

As a moped driver you will appreciate how easy the moped is to park, how it needs almost no maintenance, and how inexpensive it is to operate. In its way the moped is an ideal errand boy. A dollar's worth of gas will feed it for a week even if it's run on errands every day. A compact car will soak up ten times more gasoline running the same errands. One reason of course is the car's much larger engine. Another is that on a short run a standard automotive engine will not heat up, and will therefore operate with its choke closed. As long as the choke is closed fuel consumption will be abnormally high.

With its choke closed, the smells and poisons a car engine releases are horrendous. But even with its choke open and its temperature up, the standard auto engine produces many more fumes than the ratio of gasoline consumption may lead you to believe. The reason is the basic nature of the gasoline engine. Gas engines spew forth the least percentage of pollution at full power. Since no sane person ever runs through town at the 120 to 180 mph (193 to 290 kmh) that an auto is capable of, car engines are loafing most of the time and thereby generating an awful lot of stink. (Ever notice how badly a car smells when it is idling?) Mopeds can't loaf; they have to work their little hearts out all of the time, so they are almost always working at maximum efficiency and minimum pollution.

Mopeds aren't new. The first moped, and it really was a moped though it was called a motorcycle, was made by Gottlieb Daimler back in 1885. He was the first, so far as anyone remembers, to mount a gasoline engine on a bicycle. It worked fine, but there were no buyers. So he transferred his motor to a buggy and went on, with his partner Karl Benz, to make his fortune with the Mercedes-Benz automobile. (The company is Daimler-Benz. The car was named after Gottlieb's daughter.)

More than sixty years were to pass before anyone again mounted a gasoline engine on a bicycle and attempted to sell the combination. When they did, Europeans bought them by the trainload. The second commercial moped was first manufactured in France shortly after World War II. Called Velosolex, this vehicle had its 49-cc engine positioned above the front wheel of the bicycle, and power was transmitted from the engine by means of a rubber roller pressing on the wheel. To disengage the motor from the wheel, the motor was tilted up and back a little.

The economical French never abandoned this early design. The engine-over-wheel Solex is now manufactured by Motobecane, but the Solex is still the lightest, most efficient, and least expensive of all the mopeds presently on the market.

If you measure by the number of units made, Motobe-

cane is the largest moped manufacturer in the world, having so far produced more than twenty million mopeds. Agrati-Garelli of Italy, who has been making bicycles since 1913, and Peugeot, who has been making other things as well as bicycles since 1885, were two other early entrants in the moped industry. Now there must be almost fifty moped manufacturers in Europe alone, and to date they have produced a total of some fifty million mopeds, almost all of which are used in Europe and Southeast Asia.

There are a number of reasons for the moped's popularity overseas, but first and foremost is economy. Not only do mopeds cost far less to purchase than the smallest of cars, but also they consume a lot less gasoline, and with the high cost of gas in Europe, this is a key factor in their favor.

Mopeds were slow to travel to North America. The absence of high fuel prices in the United States and Canada and the presence of plenty of parking spaces in the cities for cars of all sizes made the moped unnecessary. The main obstacle, however, was legislative. American lawmakers refused to differentiate between motorcycles, which can easily outrun a police car, and the gentle, low-speed, low-powered moped. The moped was not outlawed, but to own and operate one you had to meet all the rules and regulations pertaining to owning and operating a motorcycle. In most states this meant a license plate and insurance for the cycle, plus passing a written and road test for the driver.

Then, in 1974, some lawmakers became convinced of the inherent safety of the moped. By 1978, thirty-two states plus the District of Columbia had recognized the moped as a distinctive breed and reregulated it accordingly. Now, in some states, you can drive a moped without any license whatsoever. In others an ordinary auto license will do. In some other states engine horsepower is the limiting requirement, and in others it is road speed. (A few states use a combination of road speed and horsepower to differentiate between mopeds and other vehicles.) Most states have a minimum age requirement. But one state, Indiana, will let you go from your crib onto a moped legally so long as the moped's engine doesn't generate more than one horsepower.

All this is discussed more fully in Chapter Five, but bear this in mind: If the moped you drive doesn't meet the requirements of the state in which it is operated, and if you don't meet its requirements either, you will be stopped and fined.

Encouraged by the new laws, the number of mopeds in the United States has grown tremendously. From less than 25,000 in 1975, their numbers will have increased to an estimated one million by the end of 1980.

## SAFETY FACTOR

Mopeds are safe. In Europe, where they have been used daily for more than thirty years, their record is far better than that of motorcycles and automobiles. There are good reasons for this. The maximum speed of a moped is only 30 mph (48 kmh), which is much less than the speed of an average automobile or motorcycle. Low speed does not guarantee safety, but experience shows it certainly helps.

The moped's low weight is another reason for its good safety record. Low weight means easy stops. In addition, modern mopeds have several times more braking surface per pound of weight than a motorcycle or an automobile.

It all adds up to a vehicle that is ultrasafe in itself. The dangers lie in the other vehicles on the road. This will be covered in Chapter Eight.

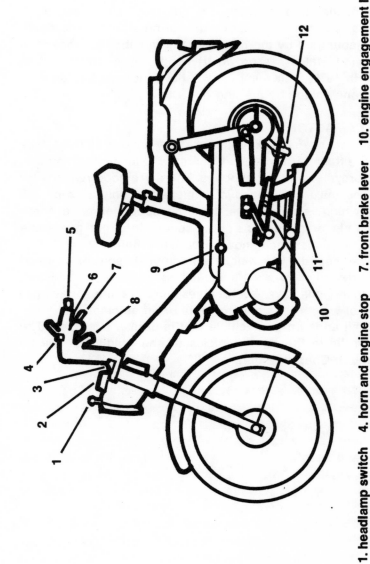

1. headlamp switch
2. speedometer
3. steering lock
4. horn and engine stop
5. decompressor control
6. throttle twist grip
7. front brake lever
8. rear brake lever
9. gas valve
10. engine engagement lever
11. kick stand
12. chain tensioner

**Usual instruments and controls on a moped.**

# 2

## *What's a Moped and How Does It Work?*

A moped is essentially a bicycle with a motor, a lightweight vehicle that travels at about the speed of a human-propelled bike and will climb most hills under its own power. (But when necessary, the mopeder helps it along by pedaling.)

Most mopeds are powered by a gasoline engine. But there are companies that manufacture electric battery and motor packages that are easily attached to a standard bicycle and can be operated as a moped. The battery can be recharged each night at home, which brings the cost of operating an electric moped down to about one tenth of a cent per mile (1.6 km). The fuel cost of operating a moped is roughly five times higher.

Mopeds will cover between 75 and 200 miles (120 and 322 km) on a single gallon of gasoline. The exact mileage your vehicle will deliver depends on its engine horsepower, your speed, the number of hills you climb, how much pedaling you do, and your own weight and size. Skinny people sitting sideways on their machines get the best mileage.

## SPEED

Maximum moped speed on a flat road is about 30 mph (48 kmh), which is a good clip on any city street or country road. However, mopeds do not have the pickup, the zip of an auto. On the average, a moped will take a good city block to reach its maximum speed on a level road. Up a slight hill, it may never reach maximum. Of course, as the grade or incline increases, your moped's speed will decrease accordingly. When you slow down to where you are just about moving, you pedal. Should you pedal too soon, there will be no resistance to your efforts, and you will know your help is not yet needed. If you wait too long, your moped will simply come to a halt, with no harm done. The motor will continue turning over. You will start to move again as soon as you start pedaling. This time you will "feel" the pedals underfoot. Should the hill become too steep, you will have to dismount and push the moped up the hill.

Downhill is a breeze. Your only problem will be restraint. You can easily hit 50 mph (80 kmh) if you don't use your brakes.

Mopeds are not designed for country lanes and dirt roads. They do not have the power to move across soft dirt, sand, mud, or deep grass. So if you are thinking about purchasing a moped for use in the deep woods, check your trails first.

## TYPES

All nonelectric mopeds have a small, two-cycle gasoline engine connected to either the front or rear wheel through an automatic transmission of one kind or another. The automatic transmission is a requirement of every state that accepts the moped as a special vehicle, and there is no doubt that this will be included in the standards of every additional state that accepts the moped in the future.

It is the automatic transmission that makes moped riding so easy. You can start the motor and forget it. The engine will continue turning over so long as you don't shut it off and there is fuel in the tank. You needn't worry about a clutch or shifting gears or stalling.

Let's assume you are waiting for a traffic light to turn green. Your right hand rests on the gas control on the right end of the handlebars. The motor is idling quietly. At this engine rpm (rotational speed), there is no firm connection between the engine and the moped wheel. Now the light changes to green. You turn the gas control to the right; the engine speeds up, and as it does it engages its load, which is simply the technical way of saying the engine starts to drive the wheel. The moped moves and you are on your way. Later, when you release the gas control (it turns to the left by itself), the engine slows down and disengages—disconnects —itself from the wheel.

Automatic transmissions can be made in a number of ways. Each manufacturer has its own idea of how this can be done best. Some use belts that slip; some use centrifugal clutches; some use wet clutches much like those used in an automobile's automatic transmission. They all work satis-factorily, but which works best is hard to tell. However, you can safely assume that if a company has been using its transmission for a number of years, that transmission is reliable.

**GEAR RATIOS**

On an auto with stick shift you select the gear ratio you wish and reverse by moving the gear selector lever. To some ex-tent you do the same thing on an automatic. Low gear gives you the pull you need to go up hills. High gear gives you the speed. Most mopeds have a fixed-gear ratio between the engine and wheels. Generally this ratio is about 15 to 1, meaning the little engine turns over fifteen times every time the wheel turns over once.

There are, however, a number of exceptions to the fixed-gear-ratio design. One is a two-speed automatic transmission that switches from high gear to low when you meet a hill and then back to high when you are back on the flats. You will find this two-speed automatic transmission on the Odyssey, Vespa Ciao, Vespa Bravo, Smily, and probably many others soon.

Another exception is a variable-ratio transmission that

adjusts itself automatically to load conditions. Depending on whether the machine is climbing a hill or rolling along on the flats, the transmission's engine-to-wheel ratio will vary from 10 to 1 to 20 to 1.

Both the two-speed and the variable-ratio transmission extend the life of the engine, increase the moped's pickup, smooth the ride, and help on hill climbing. However, there is a price to pay. Mopeds with two-speed and variable-ratio transmissions cost more, they increase the weight of the vehicle by up to 30 pounds (16 kg), and since they are more complex, they tend to require more service and more repairs.

## WEIGHT AND WHEELS

The weight of modern mopeds range from about 65 pounds (29 kg) for the Solex to a maximum of about 110 pounds (50 kg) for the largest machine. These are "dry" figures. Fuel adds a few pounds, the rider many more. Although the weight difference between the lightest and the heaviest moped is only about 45 pounds (20 kg), it is something to consider if you are planning to drag your moped into your home for safe-keeping every evening.

Standard mopeds have either 16- or 17-inch (40 or 43 cm) diameter wheels with 2¼-inch (5.7 cm) tires. There is one exception. The Solex has 19-inch (48 cm) wheels.

## STARTING SYSTEMS

Most mopeds may be started by pedaling them forward until the engine starts, which is usually at a speed a little faster than walking. Or, the moped can be placed on its kickstand, pedaled to start, then lowered to operate. To place a moped on its stand you lower the stand with your foot, then roll the machine backward. This raises the rear wheel above the ground. The moped will remain safely in this upright position by itself.

On other models you jump down on one pedal to turn it backward to start the engine. This is called a kick-start engine.

A few mopeds have spring starters. You pump the pedals

The motorscooter is another popular
motorcycle-type vehicle. Note
its smaller wheels and covered
frame. Scooters can get
almost as many miles (kilometers)
per gallon (liter) as mopeds.

backward to wind up the spring. Then the spring is released by a hand control. This is by far the best arrangement, since you can start the engine with both wheels on the ground while facing uphill.

## BOUNCE

Some mopeds have no shock absorbers. Some have shocks on their front wheel only; others have them on both the front and rear wheel. Some mount the engine on rubber and some even have extra cushions in the seat. Obviously, the more shock absorbers, the softer the ride. But how important is a soft ride? In itself not much. But the softer the ride the safer the vehicle, since the less a pothole or bump shakes up the rider, the less chance there is that he or she may lose control of the machine.

## FEDERAL STANDARDS

These are standards or regulations that apply to all mopeds on public roads, whether or not there are local moped laws. These standards set the minimum mechanical safety requirements for all motorcycles and mopeds. They are important not only because they safeguard your life, but because if your moped does not meet these standards you will be barred from riding it on public roads. Your moped must have:

•  A metal plate permanently attached to the steering post, bearing the manufacturer's name, month and year of manufacture, gross vehicle weight rating, vehicle identification number, vehicle type, and manufacturer's statement saying that the vehicle conforms to applicable regulations.

•  One adjustable sealed-beam headlight; one red tail lamp, with a double-filament bulb; one red stoplight, activated by either hand-brake control; two amber reflectors at the sides and front of the vehicle; and three red reflectors at both sides and rear of the vehicle.

•  At least one drum brake on the rear wheel, the drum to have ports through which the brake lining thickness can easily be determined.

•   Each tire must have at least six treadwear indicators so that a visual inspection will quickly determine tread depth. All tires must have a minimum tread depth of ⅟₁₆ of an inch (.16 cm). Tires must carry an identification number, size, maximum load rating in pounds (or kg), maximum inflation pressure in psi (pounds per square inch or kg/cc), maximum speed, number of plies, cord composition, and whether it is tube or tubeless.

•   There must be an engine stop on the right handlebar and it must be clearly marked as such, and its off and run positions must be indicated. There must be a manual fuel shut-off control. When in the off position this control must point forward. In the on position the control must point downward. There must be a horn and its control button must be on the left handlebar. There must be a manual choke. There must be a speedometer. Speed is to be indicated in mph or kmh and the dial must be illuminated when the headlight is turned on. There must be a rearview mirror. If it has a flat surface, that surface must be 12½ square inches (80 sq cm) or larger. If the mirror is convex, 10 square inches (64.5 sq cm) will do.

### SEE SEE'S
Mopeds have 48 to 50 cc (cubic centimeter), two-cycle gasoline engines. The figure refers to the engine's displacement, meaning the size of the work space inside the single cylinder. To give you some idea of just how small this engine is, the usual *small* lawn mower engine displaces 130 cc.

### CYCLES
Current auto engines are four-cycle jobs. This means the engine produces power every second time it turns over. A moped engine is a two-cycle job; it produces power every time it turns over, so it is a more efficient engine.

A four-cycle engine has a crankcase on its bottom that is filled with oil. A two-cycle engine does not. You never have to check engine oil when you fill your moped's gas tank. However, YOU MUST ALWAYS ADD OIL TO THE GASOLINE you use with your moped. That is the only way a two-cycle engine is lubricated. Run the engine on a tank full of pure gasoline and you will burn the engine out. The ratio of oil to gasoline varies from 1 part oil mixed with 20 parts gasoline to 1 part oil to 50 parts gasoline. The difference depends on the kind of oil and the engine design.

## COOLING

With one known exception, the Odyssey, all moped engines are air-cooled. They do not have radiators and water, and you do not have to check water level or add antifreeze in the winter. At the same time you do have to be careful not to touch the motor; it gets very hot.

## POWER AND ROAD SPEED

The power your moped engine generates depends on its design and how much gas it gets. Generally the power of any moped engine can be varied over a range of .8 to 2.2 hp (horsepower) by changing carburetors, timing, exhaust pipe, and so on. The power to which your moped has been adjusted will depend on local state rules. But obviously, the higher the hp the greater the vehicle's speed, hill-climbing ability, and gasoline consumption.

Maximum road speed on the flats depends on the gear ratio between the engine and the wheel. Naturally, you will go faster with a higher-powered engine and a wind at your back, but the basic limit is set by the gear ratio and the load the moped is carrying.

Road speed can be altered by changing the gear ratio between engine and wheels. Upping the ratio increases road speed but reduces pulling power by an equal amount. So whatever speed you may gain by doing this will be offset by loss in getaway power and hill-climbing ability.

## IGNITION

The high voltage that fires the spark in the single spark plug is generated by a magneto, which is a kind of generator. Unlike autos, which have batteries, and which always have spark power whether or not the engine is turning over, a moped's magneto supplies spark only when the engine is turning over at a fair clip.

## FUEL SUPPLY
The gas tank is always positioned above the engine so that gasoline flows into the engine's carburetor by gravity alone, as soon as you open the gas valve. When you stop the engine for more than a few minutes, the gas line valve should be closed to prevent gas loss by evaporation.

## TRANSMISSION
This is the machinery that transmits the power of the engine to the wheel. It must do several things. First, it must permit the engine to run free when you, the driver, don't want to go anywhere. Second, it must disconnect the engine when you direct your little beast up a hill it cannot climb.

If you have driven a stick-shift car you know that this disconnect action is similar to stepping on the clutch or shifting to neutral, for example, when you want to keep the engine idling while the car is standing still.

Some mopeds use a centrifugal clutch. Very simply, the motor revolves a pair of weighted, spring-loaded friction pads within a short cylinder. When the engine idles, the pads stay close to each other. When you open the throttle and feed gas to the engine and the engine speeds up, the pads fly apart and rub against the inside of the cylinder, causing it to turn with the engine. When you go up a hill and the engine is forced to slow down, the pads come together again and the motor idles freely.

A somewhat similar arrangement is used with the belt system. The belt is only engaged when the engine's speed exceeds a certain preset figure.

Still another arrangement, which is very similar to that used on automobiles, consists of two facing propellers in a tank of oil. One is connected to the engine, and as long as the engine idles the pressure on the second propeller is very low. But when the engine speeds up the pressure increases and the second propeller, connected to the wheel, is forced to turn along with the first.

## BRAKES
Moped brakes are similar to standard automobile drum brakes. The brake drum supports the wheel's spokes and is actually the hub of the rear wheel. Inside the drum there are two half-circle metal "shoes" covered with a friction-producing material. When you squeeze the brake lever, you pull on the brake cable, which forces the two shoes apart. Friction of the two shoes against the drum stops its rotation.

## LIGHTS
The lights on most mopeds are powered by magneto alone. This is the same magneto that powers the spark. When the engine slows down to idling speed, for example, when you pause a moment to speak with a friend on the sidewalk, the generated voltage drops and the lights grow dim. When you get under way once more and the engine speeds up, the lights become bright again. As you can imagine, having your headlight and taillight grow dim when you slow down or stop on a busy road is not conducive to safety.

A few mopeds are equipped with small storage batteries. The lights on these mopeds do not vary noticeably with engine speed and can be left on for a fair length of time after you have shut the engine off. Eventually, all mopeds will probably be equipped with storage batteries.

# 3

## *Which Moped?*

Any moped will do you, but some will do you better than others, so take your time and select your little beast of burden carefully. It is going to serve you a long time.

**LEGAL CONSIDERATIONS**

As stated earlier, your first legal consideration in selecting a moped is to make certain it meets federal standards, those previously described.

Your second consideration is whether or not you and the moped you select meet the state, province, and local laws that apply where you will operate your machine (even if you are just going to pass through).

In some states you can just hop aboard and take off. In others the driver must secure a license, which may require passing a written and road test. In some states mopeds run free. In others the vehicle must carry a license plate and insurance. The easy and sure way to learn all this is to write or visit the Motor Vehicle Bureau in the state or states in which you plan to ride.

## WHERE TO BUY AND WHY

Many places sell mopeds. They all guarantee their merchandise. But many of these places will direct you to the factory when you try to bring your machine back for guaranteed repairs. Since many mopeds are made in Europe, and some are even made in Taiwan, this isn't easy. So in many cases a factory guarantee is no guarantee at all.

Therefore, do not purchase your moped from a cut-rate shop. Do business with companies that deal in mopeds and motorcycles and that carry a stock of parts and have repair organizations you can actually see with your own eyes. Only such shops and companies are in a position to make the adjustments and repairs that may be due you under the terms of your guarantee.

## WHICH FEATURES?

The following are some of my own preferences based on my experience with motorcycles, mopeds, and automobiles:

• I would not select a belt drive of any kind over a centrifugal or wet (clutch) drive.

• I would always opt for the two speed over the single speed if I had the extra money and would not be troubled by the extra weight.

• I would choose the kick start over the pedal start and the spring start over the kick-start machine.

• I would choose the motor-above-the-wheel machine only after making certain I was strong enough to walk the machine easily, lift it up over curbs, and so on.

• My first choice would be the moped with the maximum hp the law allowed. It is easy enough to control your speed.

• If possible, I would select the moped with a storage battery because this would keep my lights bright all the time.

• I would not pay much attention to the size of the gas tank. One should always carry a small plastic "spare tank" of gasoline anyway.

Some moped accessories:
foldaway mirror, baskets,
saddlebags, car-carrier
equipment, and lock.

• I would spend the extra money and secure a combination speedometer/odometer (mile counter), because the odometer is the only easy way of keeping track of mileage and thereby keeping track of maintenance.

## TRY IT ON FOR SIZE

Most mopeds can be adjusted to suit the dimensions of their masters, but not all. If the moped you select cannot be made comfortable by adjusting the handlebars and seat position, don't buy it. It will not wear in, like a pair of shoes. Therefore, the first thing to do after you have found the dealer and the moped you want is to sit on it and see how it feels.

Since mopeds are costly, if the dealer will not let you ride the moped you are considering do not buy it. No matter what the vehicle laws may be in the city or village in which you are purchasing your machine, you can always operate a moped legally somewhere off the road.

In addition to sitting and actually riding the moped a short distance at least, there are certain other things you should insist upon as part and parcel of the sale. You should be given verbal instructions by the dealer on the operation, maintenance, and care of the vehicle. Never mind that you have this excellent book in hand. You should be shown everything you need to know about your machine. And the dealer or a mechanic should see that you fully understand by watching you operate the machine—start, stop, turn on the lights, and so forth.

You must receive a bill of sale clearly carrying the name and address of the seller, moped identification number, date of sale, moped description, and condition of sale (meaning what, if any, guarantee is included).

A guarantee, to be valid, must be clearly written and signed by the owner of the establishment and if a corporation, by a corporation officer. Don't buy a moped without a guarantee that includes both parts and labor. Honda, for one, gives three months or 4,000 miles free parts and labor, as do many other reliable manufacturers and their dealers. And even if the manufacturer doesn't provide a guarantee, the dealer should.

## USED MACHINES

They are "iffy" propositions at best, even if you are purchasing the machine from a friend. It is always worth the money to pay a moped mechanic to go over the moped for you before you buy it. If you buy a used machine from a dealer, make certain to get parts and labor guaranteed, or again— don't buy it.

# 4

## *Learning to Drive Your Moped*

If you now drive an automobile, you are halfway there. If you now ride a bike, you are halfway there too. And if you do both, all you need is a few minutes of instruction and a little practice to drive safely. However, if you do neither, expect to spend half a dozen hours or so learning and practicing.

### STARTING
The exact steps will vary from machine to machine, and these should be detailed in the instruction booklet and explained by the dealer selling the machine. But you may find the instructions easier to follow if you read the following first.

With the exception of the Solex and other motor-above-wheel mopeds, all the machines that have to be pedaled to start can be started on their kickstands or with both wheels on the ground. Usually, it is easier to stand the machine up on its stand.

Use your key to unlock the steering column. Open the gas valve. Pull the choke lever down or to the side, as required. Sit the moped. Push the ignition switch to ON. Place your right hand on the throttle—the right-hand grip on the handlebars. Place your left hand on the left grip, with your fingers on the compression release (or engine-engage) lever.

Now pedal the moped as you would an ordinary bike until you are going a little faster than walking speed, or at a fair clip if the moped is up on its stand. Then squeeze the compression lever against the hand grip and keep on pedaling. When you squeeze the lever you will find it more difficult to pedal, but don't slow down. This is normal and is caused by the motor that you are now turning over in addition to the moped's wheel or wheels. A few pedals later you will hear the engine catch and come to life. When this happens release the compression lever. You can stop pedaling if you wish.

The engine should now continue to idle by itself. If you believe it is going to conk out, by reason of the gasping sounds it makes, give it a little gas by turning the throttle—the grip in your right hand—a little.

Now you have the moped idling. It is either on its stand or you are holding it erect. Let it warm up for a minute or so. When it does the choke will open up by itself. There is nothing you need to do about it. Use the choke again only if you let the engine stand still long enough for it to become cold.

To start a moped having a kick-start mechanism, you begin the same way, but instead of pedaling forward, you place your weight on one pedal so as to make it turn backward. Then you jump up a little and come down with all your weight on the pedal. You don't actually kick it. With experience you can do this without troubling to put the moped up on its stand.

To start a spring-start engine you push the pedal backward a part turn a few times. This winds the spring up. Then when you are ready, you release the spring with a hand control. The spring turns the motor over and you are running.

## DRIVING

The moped's wheels are on the ground. Either you have started it this way, or you have pushed the machine forward off its stand. The stand is safely tucked out of the way.

Place both hands on the handlebar grips. Place one foot on the foot rest. The other foot remains on the ground, helping you hold the machine upright. Turn the throttle slightly to the right. This feeds more gas to the engine. The engine speeds up. The automatic clutch takes hold. You move forward, and at this moment you take your foot from the ground.

Should the machine falter at this time, you haven't given it enough gas. Give it more. If it is too late, and the machine bucks a little, release the throttle. Wait until the machine comes to a stop and put your foot down again. Now give the machine more gas this time and try again. The point here is that you want to give the engine sufficient gas to take off quickly, but not so much the little beast unseats you. After a few starts you will get the hang of it.

## TURNS

This is where previous bicycle training is invaluable. Turns are very easy, but the first time or two you may be a little hesitant to lean into a turn. The best way to gain confidence is to start your riding in a large, empty parking lot. There you can make a lot of safe, slow turns without fear or danger until you get the feel of the thing. Do not try to learn on wet ground or a dirt field; you may slip and, not being experienced, suffer a fall.

**Kick-starting a moped.
Turn the pedal backward
and then put all your
weight on it, preferably with
a little jump in the air.**

## STOPS

Remember, the REAR BRAKE MUST ALWAYS BE APPLIED FIRST; then the front brake may be applied. To make certain you never forget this, tape a block of wood beneath the front wheel brake lever so that you can't operate the front wheel brake. Note that in many instances you do not need your front brake at all.

Practice slow-speed stops, then medium-speed stops, and then medium-speed turn-stops. These are stops you make while turning in either direction. The reason for practicing these is that very often on a turn-stop the rear wheel slides to one side. Naturally, the higher the speed, the more quickly you apply the brakes, and the more the rear end will tend to swing around. Since it is only natural to try and steer away from danger when you stop, most of your panic stops will involve turning, so learn how to handle turn-stops well.

As you gain experience and confidence, increase the speeds at which you stop until you can stop smoothly from 30 mph (48 kmh) while making a panic stop. This learned, practice using your front brake along with the rear brake. Start at slow speed and work up to a two-brake stop at panic speed.

Continued practice will eventually bring you to the point where you can make panic stops using both brakes correctly without even thinking about it. Should someone step in front of you, you will make a quick, smooth stop without losing control of your moped. If all this stopping practice appears to be a waste of time, take this survivor's word for it. The few seconds you save by making a panic stop automatically can save your life.

## SHUTOFF

Move the ON-OFF switch on the right end of the handlebars to OFF. Back the machine up on its stand, and then, if you are not going to use it again shortly, close the gas valve for safety's sake and to conserve fuel. Even though the carburetor has a float valve that controls the flow of gasoline into the carburetor, when the gas inside evaporates, the float valve admits more. Gasoline vapors are dangerous. They are heavy and sink to the ground where a careless match, spark, or cigarette can ignite them.

# 5

## *Mopeds and the Law*

The accompanying table lists all the states presently taking a liberal view of the moped. These are states that do not consider the moped a motorcycle and therefore bound to all the rules, regulations, and laws restricting the operation of a motorcycle.

Unfortunately, though this table is up-to-date at this moment of writing, changes are in the legislative winds and the table will no doubt be dated shortly. However, it is a good starting point and probably will remain reasonably accurate for the states listed.

### SOME REGULATIONS

Depending on the state, you may encounter a minimum age rule, the need to pass a simple written test, the need to have a junior or senior driving license, and most states require you to license the moped. All states have a maximum speed and some have maximum engine hp limits. At least one state requires you to carry liability insurance (to pay for damages to

## CURRENT MOTORIZED BICYCLE LEGISLATION

| | CC | Power | Max. Speed | Reg. | Defined | Min. Age | License | Ins. | Helmet |
|---|---|---|---|---|---|---|---|---|---|
| Virginia | none | less than 1 bhp | 20 | no | bicycle | 16 | no | no | no |
| North Carolina | none | less than 1 bhp | 20 | no | bicycle | 16 | no | no | no |
| South Carolina | none | less than 1 bhp | 20 | no | bicycle | 12 | no | no | no |
| Texas | less than 60 | none | 20 | yes | motor-assisted bicycle | 15 | yes (written test only) | no | no |
| Ohio * | none | less than 1 bhp | 20 | no | bicycle | none | no | no | no |
| Michigan | no more than 50 | max. 1.5 bhp | 25 | yes $2.yr. | moped | 15 | any valid or moped license (no road test) | no | no |
| Nevada | none | none | 30 | no | moped | 16 | any valid | no (fin. resp.) | no |
| California | none | less than 2 gross bhp | 30 | no | mot. bicycle | 15 | any valid or learner permit | no (fin. resp.) | no |
| Hawaii | none | 1.5 bhp or less | none | no | bicycle | 15 | no | no | no |
| New Jersey | less than 50 | no more than 1.5 bhp | 25 | no | bicycle | 15 | no | no | no |
| Kansas | no more than 50 | no more than 1.5 bhp | 25 | yes $5.yr. | mot. bicycle | 14 | any valid or license w/writ. test only at 14 | no (fin. resp.) | no |
| New Hampshire | no more than 50 | no more than 2 bhp | 30 | yes $3.yr. | moped | 16 | any valid | no (fin. resp.) | no |
| Rhode Island | none | no more than 1.5 bhp | 25 | yes $10.yr. | mot. bicycle | 16 | any valid | no | no |

## CURRENT MOTORIZED BICYCLE LEGISLATION (continued)

| | CC | Power | Max. Speed | Reg. | Defined | Min. Age | License | Ins. | Helmet |
|---|---|---|---|---|---|---|---|---|---|
| Indiana † | no more than 50 | no more than 1.5 bhp | 25 | no | mot. bicycle | 15 | no | no | no |
| Maryland | less than 50 | less than 1 bhp | none stated | no | bicycle | 16 | any valid | no | no |
| Connecticut | less than 50 | no more than 2 bhp | 30 | no | bicycle | 16 | any valid | no | no |
| Arizona | 50 or less | 1.5 bhp or less | 25 | yes $8.yr. | ped. bicycle w/helper mot. | 16 | any valid | no (fin. resp.) | no |
| Iowa | no more than 50 | none | 25 | yes $5.yr. | motorized bic. or motor bic. | 14 | any valid or mot. bic. lic. at 14, no road test | no (fin. resp.) | no |
| Florida | none | max. of 1.5 bhp | 25 | no | moped, under bicycle def. | 15 | no | no | no |
| Pennsylvania | no more than 50 | no more than 1.5 bhp | 25 | yes $6.yr. | motorized pedalcycle | 16 | any valid | yes (not no fault) | no |
| Louisiana | no more than 50 | no more than 1.5 bhp | 25 | no | mot. bicycle | 15 | any valid | no | no |
| Massachusetts | no more than 50 | no more than 1.5 bhp | 25 | yes $3.—2 yrs. | mot. bicycle | 16 | any valid or learner permit | no | no |
| New York (a) | none | none | 20 | yes $5.yr. | ltd. use Class C motorcycle | 16 | any valid or special lic. | no (fin. resp.) | no |
| (b) | none | none | 21–30 | yes $5.yr. | ltd. use Class B motorcycle | 16 | any valid or special lic. | yes | yes |

| State | Weight | Horsepower | Speed | Registration | Classification | Min. Age | License | | |
|---|---|---|---|---|---|---|---|---|---|
| New Mexico | less than 50 | none | 25 | no | mot. bicycle | none stated | any valid or restricted | no | no |
| Vermont | 50 | max. 2 bhp | 30 | yes $10.yr. | moped | 16 | any valid | no (fin. resp.) | no |
| Arkansas | no more than 50 | no more than 2 bhp | 30 | no | mot. bicycle | 14 | any valid or spec. license at 14 years | no | no |
| Wash. D.C. | no more than 50 | no more than 1.5 bhp | 25 | yes $6.yr. | mot. bicycle | 16 | any valid or mot. bic. permit no road test | no (fin. resp.) | no |
| Delaware | less than 50 | no more than 1.5 bhp | 25 | yes $5.—3 yrs. | moped | 16 | any valid | no | no |
| Minnesota | less than 50 | max. 2 bhp | 30 | yes $3.yr. | mot. bicycle | 15 | any valid or mot. bic. permit | no (fin. resp.) | no |
| Tennessee | no more than 50 | no more than 1.5 bhp | 25 | no | mot. bicycle | 16 | any valid | no | no |
| Colorado | no more than 50 | no more than 2 bhp | 30 | yes $5.—3 yrs. | mot. bicycle | 16 | any valid | no | no |
| Maine | no more than 50 | no more than 2 bhp | 30 | yes $5.yr. | moped | 16 | any valid | no (fin. resp.) | no |
| Illinois | no more than 50 | no more than 2 bhp | 30 | yes $12.yr. | motorized pedalcycle | 16 | any valid | no (fin. resp.) | no |

\* Amended eff. 4/1/78: min. age 14, any valid driver's lic. or motorized bicycle license.
† Amended eff. approx. 8/31/77.

Prepared by: Motorized Bicycle Association, 1001 Connecticut Ave. N.W., Washington, D.C. 20036, August 22, 1977

the other person or property in case of an accident). And at least one state holds you liable for your vehicle. This means that if your kid sister snitches your moped and runs down your neighbor's cat, you are stuck with the cat's hospital bills—even though you locked the moped up and made certain it was safe in your garage. Your moped, your responsibility.

At least one state (New York) requires a helmet; some require annual vehicle inspection, and so on. Since these rules and regulations are changing all the time, and since you will be stopped and fined if you do not comply, check before you make a move.

### INSURANCE

Even if your state doesn't require you to carry liability insurance, you would be wise to do so. Even at low speed, you and your machine combine to form a dangerous projectile of more than several hundred pounds (90 kilograms). Should you run into someone you could cause death or serious injury. Whether the fault is yours or not, whether or not the state requires insurance or charges you with financial responsibility, you will be sued, and even if you prove your innocence beyond the proverbial shadow of a doubt, you will be stuck with legal fees.

So carry insurance and consider it a normal cost of operating a moped.

### LEGAL RIDING

A moped is a motorized vehicle. It is subject to all the road laws operative on the road you ride. You must stop for lights, you must stay on the right (or left) side of the road, you must come to a full stop at stop signs and blinking red lights, and so on.

Fail to obey the traffic laws, whatever they may be in the area you traverse, and you will risk not only a fine, but also your life. If you argue that the moped is really a bicycle, be advised that bicycles are also required to obey the same laws as motorcycles and automobiles.

Be further advised that mopeds are not automatically permitted wherever bicycles and automobiles are permitted. In some areas you cannot drive a moped down a bicycle path, and many states and counties are banning mopeds on highways with posted speeds of 50 mph (80 kmh) or more.

# 6

## *Moped Maintenance*

Maintenance is what you do to keep a thing running for a long, long time. In the case of mopeds, you don't need to do much. But the small amount that is necessary is *very* necessary.

### OILING THE GAS
Each manufacturer specifies what they believe is best for their engine in the matter of oil-to-gasoline ratio and the kind of oil to use. If they call for two-stroke oil or synthetic oil, they are talking about a special kind of oil made for moped engines. Generally, with this kind of oil the ratio is 1 part oil to 50 parts gasoline, which is usually specified as regular, unleaded gasoline.

As first choice use the oil recommended or made by the moped maker. As second choice any of the special moped oils available may be used. There is Bell-Ray's new synthetic oil called MC1, Klotz Techniplate, Castrol two-stroke, and the formula sold by Puch (pronounced Pook) for use with their machines.

As third choice you can use any two-stroke oil made for motorcycles and outboard engines.

When there is nothing else, you can use automobile oil. The heavy-duty detergent oils are the best. The 10-30 all-weather oils are less desirable than the pure oils.

When you use an auto oil or an oil not made specifically for moped engines, use a ratio of 1 part in 30 for two-cycle oil and 1 part in 20 for automobile oil.

Some mopeds have gas tank caps that are to be used as measuring devices. When the gas tank is filled with gas, the cap is filled with oil, inverted, and screwed in place. This is not an accurate means of mixing, because the ratio between cap and fuel is only accurate when the tank is empty. A more accurate method consists of mixing the oil and fuel in a separate container and then pouring the mixture into the tank. Better yet, purchase a moped with automatic oil injection.

The following tables will help you secure the oil-gas ratio you need:

1 gallon contains 128 liquid ounces
1 part in 50 means you add 2.56 ounces of oil
1 part in 30 means you add 4.3 ounces of oil
1 part in 20 means you add 6.4 ounces of oil to 1 gallon of gasoline.

*or*

1 liter contains 1,000 cubic centimeters
1 part in 50 means you add 20 cc of oil
1 part in 30 means you add 33 cc of oil
1 part in 20 means you add 50 cc of oil to each liter of fuel.

Use a standard measuring cup for the oil. If the cup is marked off in ounces, and you need cc's, figure every liquid ounce equals 30 cc's, and you will be close enough.

If you add too much oil to the gasoline your cylinder and plug will foul up more quickly than usual. If you use too little oil, wear is accelerated. It isn't too much of a job to take a single-cylinder engine apart and remove the carbon. A worn engine, however, is a junk engine.

## DRIVE CHAIN

Once a week or at least every 300 miles (480 km) or so, check the drive chain—the one connected to the engine and not the pedals—for slack. Lift the chain at its midpoint with your finger, and if you can raise the chain more than the thickness of your finger, tighten it to where you cannot raise it more than half this distance. But under no circumstance should the chain be made so tight there is no slack at all. To do so would put a strain on the chain and sprockets, wearing them out quickly, and would also put a drag on the engine, slowing it down.

To tighten the chain, loosen the two rear-wheel axle nuts. Your next step depends on the system used on your moped to position the rear axle. If you own a Motobecane 50L or 50S, or a similar machine, just pull the wheel back and retighten the axle nuts.

On machines like the Flandria 104, you will see the same slot in which the axle is free to move (when the nuts are loosened), but in addition you will find bolts within the slots. Tighten these bolts to draw the rear wheel away from the motor and so tighten the chain. Then retighten the axle bolts.

Some machines, such as the Garelli, have spiral metal guides on the rear axles. After loosening the set screws, these guides are turned to move the axle.

But no matter what system is used, the steps you need to take to move the axle should be obvious once you examine it.

Taking up on the drive chain is very simple, but you must beware of two things: making the chain too tight, as mentioned, and moving the rear wheel out of line. To keep the wheel centered, measure from the sides of the rear wheel to the sides of the frame before you retighten the axle nuts, and adjust the wheel as necessary.

**To take up the drive chain,
first loosen the rear-axle nuts.**

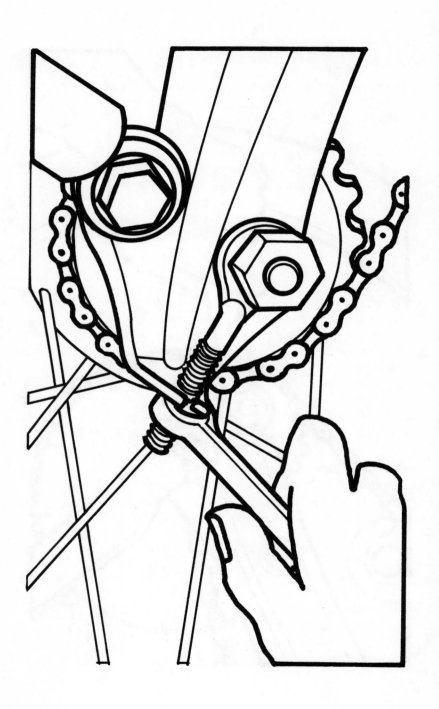

Chains are generally lubricated every week, as stated, by means of a few drops of oil on each and every link. Any heavy oil will do. Apply the oil at night, and place a long rag beneath the chain to catch the drips. Then wipe the excess from the chain in the morning.

## GEARBOX

Assuming your moped has one, follow the manufacturer's instructions and check its oil level about once every 1,000 miles (1,600 km). Make it your habit to run your hand over the bottom of the gearbox every now and then to make certain no oil is leaking out. If it is, tighten the screws and bolts. If it continues to leak, you will have to replace the gaskets.

## TIRES

Most moped tires have tubes, just like auto tires used to. The tire's carcass is made like an auto tire and is very strong. Since speed and weight are low, you can expect your moped tires to run thousands of miles before they need replacement. They won't puncture unless you run over a nail.

Since moped inner tubes are made of synthetic rubber they don't leak air, so in theory all you need do is glance at them once in a while to make certain you are not running them "bald," meaning there is little tread left.

In practice, however, it is a good idea to squeeze each tire affectionately each day before you take off. A soft tire does not turn over as easily as a hard tire; it drags. This reduces moped speed, and engine mileage and life. A very soft tire can come off its rim while you ride.

**Then move the wheel away from the motor by adjusting the axle-positioning device. In this case, the nut on the bolt holding the axle is being tightened.**

Also check tire pressure with a gauge every now and then, early in the morning while the tires are cold, just to make certain the tires are not only hard, but properly inflated. Generally, front tires are operated at 26 psi (1.8 kg) and the rear tires are inflated to 32 psi (2.2 kg).

See the following chapter for tips on removing wheels.

### TRANSMISSION
Each transmission requires its own special maintenance. A wet clutch transmission generally needs no more than keeping its oil level up to the mark. Belt transmissions should be kept clean and dry, which means that you do not let your moped stay out in the rain or play in dirt or sand. Most transmissions require a few drops of oil here and there. See your instruction manual and make certain you oil these fittings or bearings. It is important these spots be lubricated as directed.

### AIR FILTER, EXHAUST, GENERAL LUBRICATION
Clean the air filter every 300 miles (480 km) or every week. Do not ride without the filter in place. The engine can be damaged.

Clean the exhaust every month or every 1,000 miles (1,600 km) or so. A clogged exhaust will slow the engine down and decrease gasoline mileage.

As for general lubrication, each machine is different. See your instructions. If you have lost yours, just put a drop of oil on each moving joint once a month or so.

**To replace a taillight bulb, first remove the light's cover with a screwdriver. The old bulb can then be taken out by pressing it inward and turning it to the left.**

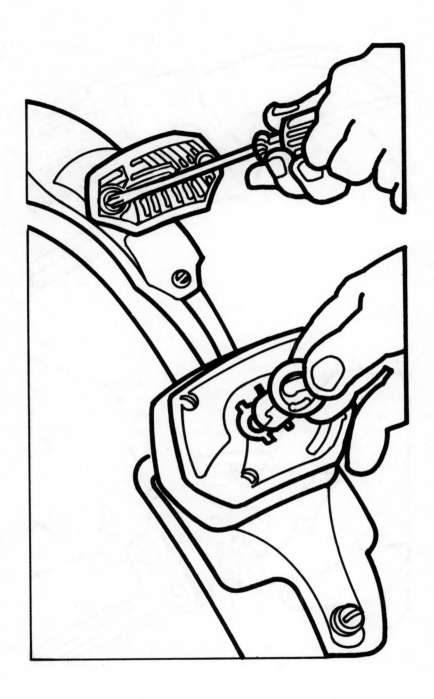

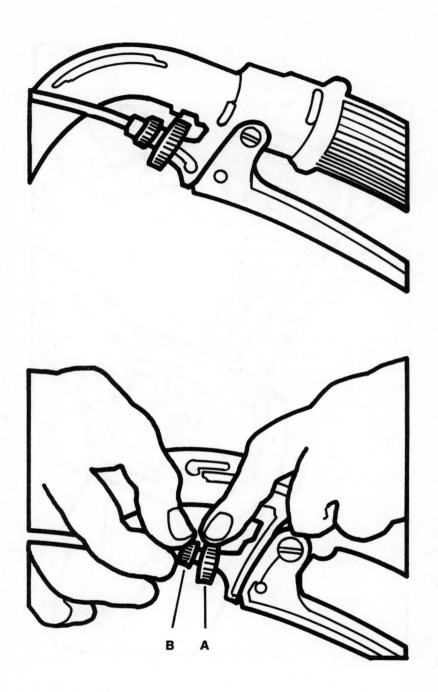

B A

## BRAKES

As the brakes wear you will find you have to press the brake levers closer and closer to the grips to stop the moped. When the tip of the lever is one inch (2.5 cm) from the grip, it is time to adjust the brake cable.

Lift the moped up on its kickstand. Loosen the large nut at the lever end of the rear wheel brake cable. Turn the small nut (milled ferrule) until you can operate the brake by moving the lever one-half inch (1.25 cm) or so. Spin the rear wheel to make certain it is free. Test the brake. Tighten the large nut.

Now do the same with the front wheel brake cable. Roll the moped or have someone lift the front wheel and spin it to make certain it is free before you tighten the large nut.

## AXLES AND BATTERY

Once a month take a wrench to the nuts on the front and rear axles to make certain they are tight.

If your moped has a storage battery, test its charge with a hydrometer once a month. If the charge remains consistently low, or worse yet, consistently high, have the charging rate corrected.

Keep the water level up. Wash the top of the battery with plain water every time it shows a little crud. No oil or grease should be placed on the connections.

**To tighten the brake cable, loosen the large nut (A) first. Then turn the small nut (B) as much as necessary. Finally, tighten the large nut.**

# 7

## *Moped Repairs*

The following are repairs or long-term maintenance adjustments that you can do with ordinary tools and without any special automotive experience.

### FLAT TIRE
The chance of getting a flat tire on your moped is far less than the chance of getting one on a car, so there is little point in buying and carrying tire-repair tools. But you should know how to remove a wheel so that you can bring it into a garage.

To remove the front wheel, disconnect the brake cable at the drum on the wheel. Loosen the axle nuts and slide the wheel off.

To remove the rear wheel, loosen the axle nuts, disconnect the brake cable, vary the axle-positioning gadgets to bring the wheel close to the engine. Then slip the chain or belt off, and you can remove the wheel.

## SPARK PLUG

To remove the plug you need a socket wrench of the correct size. Do not use pliers or a crescent wrench; you will crack the plug.

It is much better to replace a dirty plug than to clean it, but if you have no replacement, use a small knife to clean it off.

To gap the plug, and this is important, measure the space between the wire ends with a wire gauge, and then bend the little arm as necessary. Gap spacing is fairly critical, so follow the manufacturer's instructions faithfully.

## DECARBONIZING

Every 25,000 miles (40,000 km), or so they say, the inside of the cylinder will have collected so much carbon you will feel a drop in power and notice an increase in fuel consumption. (A word to the wise: If you don't feel it, ignore it.) The cure, if carbon deposits are the trouble, is to remove the carbon.

Purchase an engine head gasket and gasket cement. Remove the ignition wire and plug. Remove the head bolts or nuts. Tap the head gently until it comes off, or turn the engine over with the plug in place and NO IGNITION. With the head off, use a putty knife or butter knife to gently scrape the carbon free. Blow the engine clean. DO NOT USE STEEL WOOL OR SANDPAPER. Remove the old head gasket. Clean the surface. Apply a little cement. Position the new gasket and then the head. Replace the bolts. Tighten each just a little at a time, so that they are all made equally tight at almost the same time. DO NOT OVERTIGHTEN. Replace the plug and ignition wire and you are done.

Do not try to do anything else to the engine and transmission unless you have the proper tools and plenty of experience.

## BRAKES

When you have taken up on the brake cables as much as you can, you will have to adjust the brake shoes within their drums to make the brakes work properly again. Start by

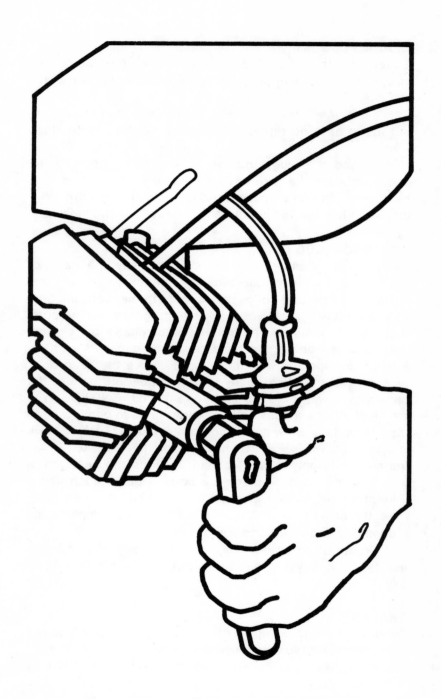

**Use a socket wrench to remove the spark plug.**

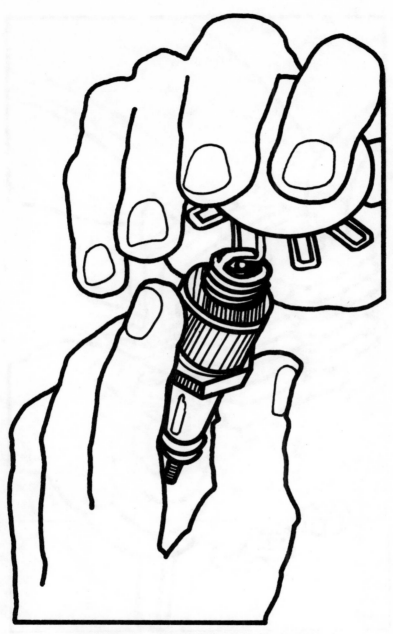

Do not guess at the spark plug gap; use a
wire gauge to measure the point separation, as
shown. Bend the side electrode as required.

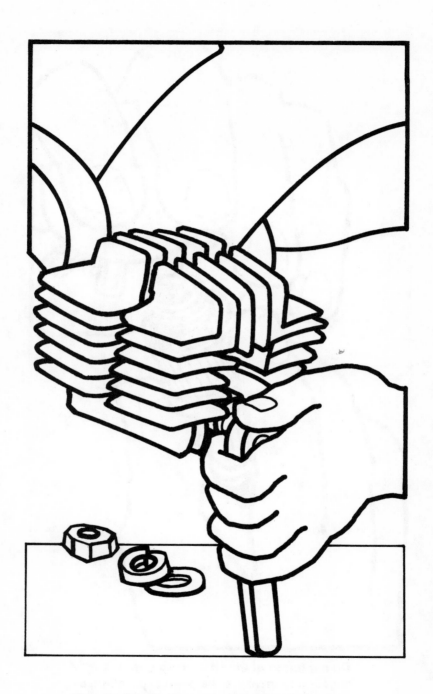

To decarbonize the cylinder, first remove the
nuts or bolts holding the cylinder head in place.
But do this *after* removing the spark plug.

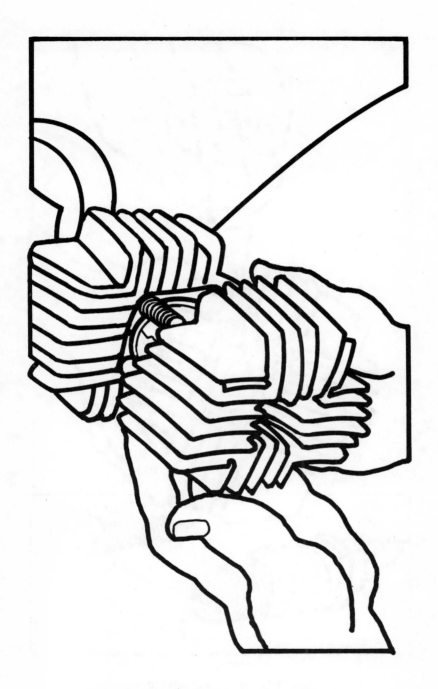

**Next, carefully remove the cylinder head.**

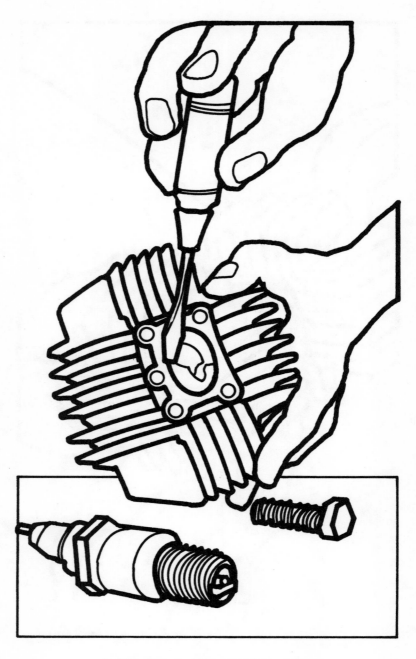

**Third, remove the carbon from the
cylinder head with a worn screwdriver or similar dull-edged tool.**

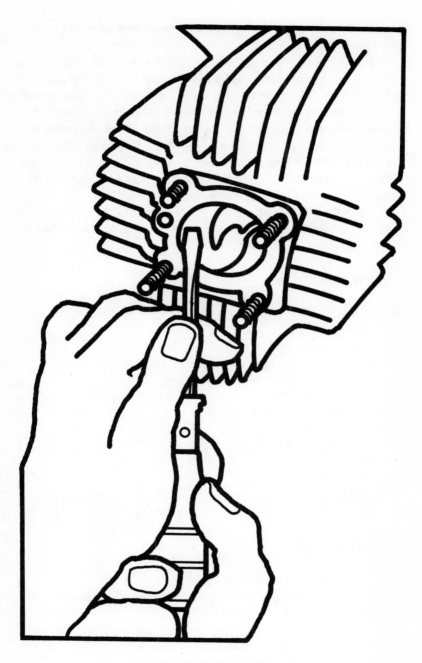

**Then use the same tool to clean the top of the piston.**

loosening the large nuts on the control end of the cables; then back the small nuts off as far as you can.

Put the moped on its stand. Go to the drum end of the rear wheel brake cable. Loosen the locknut and turn the other nut or adjustment while you revolve the rear wheel by hand. When you cause the wheel to stop you know the brake shoe has touched the inside of the drum. Reverse the small nut or adjustment three turns. The wheel now runs free. Go to the control end of the rear brake cable and adjust the two nuts there until you can work the brake by moving the lever about one-half inch (1.25 cm).

To adjust the front brake, have someone hold the front end of the moped up in the air while you work. It is adjusted exactly like the rear wheel brake.

## TROUBLESHOOTING

### Won't start:

See that there is fuel in the tank.
See that the gas valve is in the open position.
See that the ignition switch is ON.
See that the ignition wire is connected to its plug.
See that the plug is not cracked.
See that the plug and ignition wire are dry.
See that the air filter is not clogged.
See that the choke is in its closed position if the engine is cold.
If the engine is hot (having run before) and won't start, wait until it is cold, close the choke, and try again.

### Difficult to start:

See that the spark plug is not cracked.
See that the plug's gap is correct and the plug is clean.
See that the wire to the plug is dry.
See that the plug is dry.
See that the air filter is clean and in place.

See that there is gas in the tank.
See that nothing interferes with the choke.
See that the exhaust is not clogged.
If necessary, try turning the throttle a little when starting.

**Rough idling:**

See all of the above.
See that the wires to the ignition switch are tight.
See that the carburetor is not loose.

**Rough running:**

Check the spark plug by replacing it.
Clean the gas filter if there is one.
Drain gas; it may contain water or dirt.
See "Rough idling" and "Difficult to start," above.

**Lack of power:**

See that the tires are fully inflated.
See that the brakes are not dragging.
Check plug by replacing it.
See that the air filter is not clogged.
See that the exhaust is not clogged.
Clean the gasoline filter if there is one.
See that the gas valve is in the full open position.
Spin the wheels to see that bearings are properly lubricated.
See that the drive chain or belt is not too tight.
See that you haven't gained a lot of weight.

**Engine overheats:**

Add a little oil to the gasoline immediately.
See that the air filter is in place.
Check out everything suggested above.
See that your clothing or packages are not interfering with
    the passage of air over the engine.

# 8

## *Driving Safely*

Mopeds are not dangerous in themselves. Neither are cars or trucks or bicycles. But mix them all up together with a few dogs, cats, and pedestrians, and lots can happen—some of it bad.

To be safe you must be constantly conscious of danger. You cannot forget yourself. This does take the edge out of a lot of our activities, but there is no other way to stay in one working piece. Drop your guard for a moment and you can be in serious trouble. So accept the presence of danger. Prepare for it by always wearing suitable clothing. This means a crash helmet and sturdy shoes and reasonably heavy clothing. Don't ride your beast bareheaded and barefooted. If you do, the slightest spill can cause you considerable injury.

Always make it your practice to check your moped before taking off for the day's fun. This means trying the brakes; squeezing the tires to see if there is sufficient air; pushing the wheels sideways to see if the axle nuts are tight and there isn't excessive play in the bearings.

## Run with your lights on
In some states it is illegal to operate a motorcycle day or night without its headlight and taillight turned on. This is a very good law and one you should abide by. Mopeds are not particularly large or noisy machines. Running with your lights on makes you that much more visible and therefore that much safer.

## Don't drive at dusk, at night, or in the rain
Dusk is a very bad time because there is so much skylight that it is difficult for us to see things on the ground. This time of day has been and still is a peak time for accidents. Night isn't much better, because motorists are often blinded by oncoming lights. They also tend to doze off and to confine their attention to the road immediately in front of them. There are also more drunks out on the road at night, and fully one half of all the driving fatalities involves one or more drunken drivers. And late at night you meet the speed demons, drivers who believe they are running the Daytona 500. Most auto deaths occur late at night, despite the limited number of vehicles on the road.

Your own sight is also severely restricted at night. You cannot see small obstructions on the road such as bottles and sticks lying about. You will not see potholes or water and oil slicks. Things that are harmless during the day can easily ruin you at night merely because you cannot see and thus avoid them.

Visibility is low and traction is poor in the rain. You may skid, the auto may skid, and the moped will get wet. Mopeds do not like to get wet. By the same token you should not ride in the snow, although mopeds do not dislike snow as much as they dislike rain.

## Obey the law
The legal need to obey the law was mentioned earlier on. That is only one reason. Another is your own safety. If you

slip across intersections against the light, if you do not obey the signs, you will sooner or later suffer an accident.

### Trust no one
Assume that other drivers will not obey the lay. Sometimes—too many times—they do not. Do not take it for granted the car approaching a stop sign will stop, or that no one is going to run a red light.

### Stay on your portion of the road
Do not wander all over the road. Hold to as straight a line as you can. If you are making a left turn, stay on the right-hand side of the road all the way around the turn. Do not cut it short. When on a country road, do not assume no one is coming in the opposite direction. You won't hear cyclists and a bike can be almost as damaging as a car.

### You can't be seen
You may find this hard to believe, but there are positions in relation to automobiles and especially trucks and buses where you will be invisible to the driver. There are two blind spots to the rear and side of an auto where even an oncoming car is not in the car's mirror. You will be invisible to the driver of a bus or truck if you are immediately in front of the vehicle or along its sides. Most of the time a driver of a big truck will look right over your head without actually seeing you or being consciously aware of you.

You must therefore make it your business to stay clear of all vehicles and to bear in mind the possibility that the truck or auto ahead of you will make a turn and cut you off. You must give yourself lots of space when you are behind a car or truck because it can stop faster than you can, and you may run into it when it does.

### Don't switch lanes in traffic
Since a moped is far more maneuverable than a car or truck, some foolish mopeders take advantage of their agility in slow-moving traffic to better their position on the road. Not only does this anger other drivers, but should the traffic

suddenly speed up, you will very likely be knocked down. One reason is that you are partially invisible as you move between cars and trucks. Another is that none of the drivers even consider the fact you cannot accelerate as fast as they can and cannot reach their speed. For a little while you and your moped are like a rabbit among turtles, then suddenly, you become a turtle, the cars and trucks become rabbits, and you get hopped on.

Stay in your lane. Stay clear of fast-moving and slow-moving traffic. Stay where you can be seen and where you can, should the situation call for it, escape into the gutter or onto the shoulder of the road.

### Get clear before you turn
On right turns get all the way over to the right before turning. On left turns get all the way over to the left. Do not make your turn until there is no one coming in the opposite direction who is going to challenge you, but wait, with your hand clearly outstretched indicating your purpose, until the road is clear.

### Beware the big winds
Prepare to be pushed a little to the side when a big truck or bus speeds past you. Remember that at speeds of above 30 mph (48 kmh) most of the engine's effort goes to move the air out of the way. So there is always a big wind accompanying a large, fast vehicle.

### Watch those two-lane roads
Should you find yourself alongside an auto on a two-lane road, and there is another car coming in the opposite direction, estimate its speed carefully. If there is a chance the two cars will be side by side while you are alongside one car, slow down. Do not permit yourself to be the third vehicle on the road. Many drivers move to their right when faced with oncoming traffic on a narrow road. They will push you into a ditch. They are not afraid of running into mopeds, but the thought of a head-on collision unnerves them and they unconsciously move away.

**Parked cars can be dangerous**
Do not drive close to the sides of parked cars. Many drivers break the law and leave their cars from the road side of the vehicle. Should they open their door while you are passing, the results will not be pleasant.

Good luck.

# *Index*

# *About the Author*

Max Alth has written
*All About Bicycles and Bicycling,*
*All About Motorcycles,* and
*How to Keep Your Car Alive,*
among other books.
He has been an editor
on the staff of the magazine
*Automobile International*
and is currently at work on
a book about World War II.

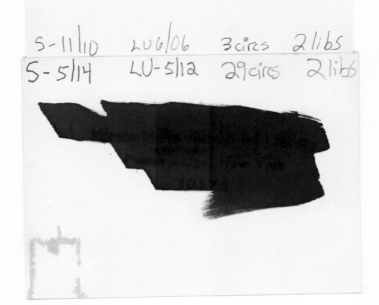